Oyama Pink Shale

Oyama Pink Shale

Sharon Thesen

poems

ANANSI

Copyright © 2011 Sharon Thesen

All rights reserved. No part of this publication may be reproduced or transmitted in any form or by any means, electronic or mechanical, including photocopying, recording, or any information storage and retrieval system, without permission in writing from the publisher.

This edition published in 2011 by
House of Anansi Press Inc.
110 Spadina Avenue, Suite 801
Toronto, ON, M5V 2K4
Tel. 416-363-4343
Fax 416-363-1017
www.anansi.ca

Distributed in Canada by
HarperCollins Canada Ltd.
1995 Markham Road
Scarborough, ON, M1B 5M8
Toll free tel. 1-800-387-0117

Distributed in the United States by
Publishers Group West
1700 Fourth Street
Berkeley, CA 94710
Toll free tel. 1-800-788-3123

House of Anansi Press is committed to protecting our natural environment. As part of our efforts, this book is printed on paper that contains 100% post-consumer recycled fibres, is acid-free, and is processed chlorine-free.

15 14 13 12 11   1 2 3 4 5

LIBRARY AND ARCHIVES CANADA CATALOGUING IN PUBLICATION

Thesen, Sharon, 1946–
Oyama pink shale / Sharon Thesen.

Poems.
ISBN 978-0-88784-272-6

I. Title.

PS8589.H433O92 2011   C811'.54   C2010-906477-1

Library of Congress Control Number: 2010940728

Cover design: Bill Douglas
Typesetting: Marijke Friesen

We acknowledge for their financial support of our publishing program the Canada Council for the Arts, the Ontario Arts Council, and the Government of Canada through the Canada Book Fund.

Printed and bound in Canada

        not to see anymore

but inward

      not to know   but

your own self

        sealed

        sealed

o

        sea

            with no tide

                    — Etel Adnan

Contents

Five Preludes 1
Interior, Postwar 6
The Bracelet 13
Shuswap Lake 14
Alphabets 15
A Sunday Drive 16
Ripple Rock 17
Party Nights 19
The Fishing Trip 20
Anaïs Nin 21

Robbie King 22
The Month of March 23
The Consumptives at Tranquille
        Sanitorium, 1953 24
Oyama Pink Shale 30
The Mummy Suite 31
The World 34
The Big Top 35
The Nets of Being 36
Lines 45
Queen of the North 47
The Middle of August 48

February   49
Life Studies   50
The Torturer's Horse   51
A Lovely Day   52
White Hillside   53
Death in the Moonlight, a Sinking Canoe   55
From Toledo   56
The Shepherdess   59

Notes and Acknowledgements   63
About the Author   67

Five Preludes

I.

Someone about to go back to the hotel room
was thinking about her hat, actually,
two hats. She would put on
the grey hat or the green hat.
She was a different person in the green hat,
more open-minded. Not a hummingbird
green but a black green like the North Shore.
In the grey hat she had less patience
and a stone sat between her legs.
She could already see herself putting
the blue card in the door handle, the green
light flash once. She would reach into the
closet shelf where the hats lay side by side
like those who died for Truth and Beauty in
Dickinson's poem & choose one in *agnosia*,
in darkness, and descend to the town's
winter sales past the gentle cemetery greyly
gleaming in *Phoebus'* gentle rays.

2.

Someone about to climb a hill
decides to take the animals' path
instead of the beaten track
but soon it takes certain dark turns
amid crowding trees below radioactive
cliffs of Oyama pink shale & seems to narrow
and grow vague, vague as the perorations of
greybeards like herself in the academies of Yes
and of Total Access, she herself an open door
but more, the light it sheds across the carpeting
a parallelogram containing the shade of W. B. Yeats
whom Ireland couldn't contain, nor the weather.
What have we now but a wall of younger granite, slate-blue
& crumbling like the ziggurats of yore, and is this
battened-down place in the bunchgrass the animals'
bedroom? Breathless now, her green hat folded in her pocket
she backs down and away, as if condemned at the docket.

3.

Someone about to go to an event
was wondering if she should have some pistachios first or wait.
If she waited, she might keel over and then what.
The evening would bore on like an auger drill
that digs into heartwood & sends up spirals of fragrant
beige curls. While standing in her boudoir
Flight 246 passed overhead & her socks
left crimps in the flesh of her ankles betraying
last-minute preparations as she crosses naked shins
in the armchair of absentia, of the lamentations
catalogued in the catalogue of Malcolm Lowry's personal effects:
charred manuscripts and a photograph of an old ginger cat.
Buckles up her sandals like a Greek bust with tidy coif,
a spray of Mitsouko and then they're off.

4.

Someone about to make a tomato sandwich
opens the fridge door and reckons the laden racks,
the many jars and misty tubs
below, caress of parsley, smear of red pepper
like a goldfish, the *poisson rouge*
of Matisse's paintings in which three to five
dwell in a glass bowl beside an
odalisque reading a novel or writing a letter.
Dear Malcolm, it says, I shall never forget
the afternoon we spent on the mudflats
picking up kelp & seashells in our bathing suits.
I beg you, be careful! The fish flit, blips
of orange hue, transparent fins undulant
& aloft, beautiful things,
and all of them — fish, Malcolm, odalisque —
far away from the Roundup
and technologies courtesy of Krupp.

5.

Someone about to be thrown out the door by Ernest Hemingway
adjusts his hat, later to apologize by special
delivery. Not a brighter sun could infuse the world
with blueness and whiteness than the one that lit
this palm-tree-shaded event. She came across it on Wikipedia,
consternation deepening the lines inscribed in her cheeks &
radiating from the corners of her orbs like the gills of Dogfish
    Woman
resurrected from under the grey seas of Haida Gwaii
— this shocking event in the "quiet, uneventful life" of Wallace
    Stevens.
Such a fracas could lead a person permanently astray, throw him
out the window of time and space, like the esemplastic power of the
imagination which was ignited in Stevens by the first sightings,
on a regular basis, of the Florida Keys,
which could just about send him to his knees.

Interior, Postwar

Graphite

Sweet as the scent at the sawmill where Mur would glean
a scrap for the winter stove, pencil wood coiled
out one end of the sharpener, a fine point out the other.

Smoke rose from Mur's ashtray
& from the beehive burner
where the vet cremated dead pets,

a terrible procession on certain nights advancing the corpses
to the lip of the hive. Fire hot as a nebula
tossing new suns out the screen nub at the top

while Mur added up long sums,
pencil point barely touching the digits
swift down the list & carrying the two,

fine dotted leavings of calculations
alongside the debits and credits.
Who owed who what and what for

was secret in the heart of Mur
whose genuine handshake bore the charcoal dust
of bark-wood subtracted from an over-stuffed stove

and laid on a mat smoky hot and groaning,
leaving a log-shaped desert of rosy coals brightening.

Next Door

The burlwood coffee table an amazement of the former tree itself
bulbous and jolly, shiny & amber,

whose warped and wavering rings
are so many the lines blur our reckonings

every time we arrive *en famille*
for a smorgasbord Danish-style,

Mrs. Rasmussen having cooked for days, the house
immaculate

in a dim and ticking Old World way gleaming with
candlesticks beer mugs rose-coloured shot glasses for the Akvavit

intricate numerous courses all afternoon
until us kids go down to count the burlwood rings

& fool around and in the early darkness out the window
a spruce's lugubrious branches slightly swayed &

the tenant's afternoon-shift torso innocently passed by
unshot at,

the mill finished with tree trunks for Saturday
more stacked up in the yard or coming down

in daring switchback javelin loads the night shift looks after

— *here you're free,*
you make money, it's paradise.

Ice Skating

Mrs. Takahashi's tiny brown house
seemed to disappear at twilight

her widow hoe furrowed rows & quietly
in her crops she squatted and weeded

asparagus and sky-high beans,
traded with nods silvery dried seaweed

with my mother, a connoisseur
of ocean's bounty from being raised

on halibut and clams, unimaginable to both of them

this arid zone where we skated in the wind
on frozen fields made of shallow puddles

my new friend from the Old Country
& I, on ridged and tattered ice

soft yellow weeds poked through
to halt your blades —

she landed on one arm
& hearing the crying
her mother ran out from Warsaw or Danzig —

I mimed my friend's route,
her falling, my wanting her to know
I had done nothing to hurt her child.

Novelty Items

Salt 'n pepper shakers in the cupboard above the stove.
A girl with yellow hair and long red skirt, a boy in blue shorts.
She has numerous holes in her head, he has two.

The furnace cuts in, bathroom fan shrieks,
snow piles up six feet outside the back door.

Bacon slices make gentle waves of themselves in the pan,
heat turned down, a gentle sizzle

Wafts upward to the good girl-and-boy in the cupboard above,
Hitler-Jugend, she more used than he, being salt

and he, being pepper, peppered more often than she
and so a lack of he's, and many she's, being used

Being used and dying, peppered and dead, between them
used, half used, dead, and dying, & with tear-salted cheeks

rosy, creamy, and round.

Birdbath

The birdbath bowl lies separate from its torso
archaic in pine-needle-draped Oyama shale

ever awaiting a hopeless dream of restoration and return
to its spot in the centre of the front lawn

where George, returned from the Merchant Marine
& fresh from deep unspoken wounds of battle

in the far seas of the Polynesian archipelagos
far, far off the coasts of Australasia

the sky in sudden murderous brightnesses shocking
the dark, shiny, romantic waves of evening

into which fell burning the smokestacks, the ships, the men
in their uniforms still holding rifles and life-vests

filled it every morning. Tweeting &
cheeping filled the innocent nearby cedar-scented shrubbery

and the chickadees would wait to land on the curves
of the bowl's sloshing scalloped edges

until George, seasick, would go back in the house,
take an aspirin, and rue the truths of his reflection
in the silver curves of the coffee pot.

The Bracelet

From the Queen Charlottes my mother's uncle sent
cans of crabmeat and Haida silver bracelets.
Mine was signed "XX" inside. Dogfish Woman

appears a bit slapdash, off at an angle — XX's poetics
of slapdash and on-an-angle amidst the TB
and the whalers and the moieties

Dogfish Woman looks out toward the future, Raven's
wing behind her on the port side of the Black Canoe,
the labret in her bottom lip eclipsing the sea, her

Wonder Woman tiara flashing like a lighthouse in the wrath
of the Straits of Hecate and the ruin of Prince William Sound.

Shuswap Lake

Swaths of sunbeams fell
through warm shadows astringent
with the green waxy odour
of willow & poplar, through cedar boughs
and the cloaks of angelic presences
& it's true that in that holy grove plants & animals
consumed one another in fear and pain.
The trickling of a stream, whump
of a raven's wing I lingered among,
awhile. Then we did stunts, leapt
from the woodshed roof or some dirt pile
atop which we wrestled & strove murderously
to make a drama: we'd call Mom
to watch us knock ourselves out
like the epigraph to *The Great Gatsby*:
"Then wear the gold hat if that will move her;
if you can bounce high, bounce for her too"

& even now, fairly often, I think "boats against the current"
or boats "beating back against the current"
when in traffic from the novel's lyrical conclusion.

Alphabets

Astride their smaller versions, capital letters
cantered above Mrs. Humphrey's blackboard.
Unbelievably, my friend Barbara's parents owned
a candy store accessed from their house by a stone
footbridge in the moonlight.

And in the park I pumped the swing almost
to going overbars and had to go here and there
in the backseat of the stifling car to the outlying areas on
     Sunday visits

And laughed to hear the name "Mrs. McGillicuddy"
spoken while picking peas and when walking by saw
the axe yanked from the stained tree stump
in the chicken yard and a terrified one
dashing around being reached out for.

A Sunday Drive

Dogfish Woman flashes by in the Black Canoe
crowded, said Bill Reid, as a Sunday afternoon drive
in the station wagon with the dog. In the back seat
we fought secretly & openly either side of the line
down the centre of the back seat. *Shut up
back there* said Dad, *I'm trying to drive! Stop that
right now* said Mom *or else!* I'd been shown harnesses
and small buckles and a box of snow-white
rectangles with handles like a hammock that went
between your legs. The labret of Dogfish Woman
protrudes and meets the lowest tip of her hooked nose.
She looks ahead out of eyes with the vertical pupils
of her salmon relatives. No other lifetime could match
living in the far depths with the sharks,
having laughed at their double penises
when washed up dead on the beach. Dogfish Woman
is different now, she has the scars to prove it, the gills
high on her cheekbones, the power of her stroke.

Ripple Rock

For a long time we'd been waiting for the day
we could watch Ripple Rock blow up on TV

on stick legs it sat in the living room,
Bishop Fulton J. Sheen and *I Love Lucy* pre-empted.

Lucy always had good intentions, but things got out of control —
her battle was with the intransigence of the material world

& so was Bishop Fulton J. Sheen's.

On the TV screen, the ordinary waters of Seymour Narrows,
a voice-over narrating the history of Ripple Rock —
a twin-peaked underwater mountain —
& bemoaning the ships, boats, and Sunday
pleasure craft it had wrecked. Enough was enough,
"Old Rip" had to go.

Like communism Ripple Rock hid
nine feet below surface at low tide. Ripple Rock in the
church hall, Ripple Rock in the highball, Ripple Rock
in the square-dance call.

We gazed upon the face of the deep.

A lazy current swirled around the sleeping
innocent peaks — innocent as Lucy
dead to the world in her big pyjamas,
white cold cream on her cheeks, kerchief holding curlers in place

and finally a cracking roar of rock, dust, and smoke
as bits & pieces of Ripple Rock
fell back down into the Narrows

& sadness befell us for the hauling out
of the busted underworld into fuming light of day.

Party Nights

Bacardi, rye-and-sevens, Ritz crackers, rollmops,
coils of garlic sausage, smoked oysters from the Queen Charlottes,
a reverent silence as Dad took the five-string banjo
out of the black case, laid the strap over his shoulder
and lit into "Ragtime Cowboy Joe."

On winter afternoons by 4:00 it was dark.
So it would have been dark already for four or five hours.
Overshoes piled up in the doorway, coats on the bed.
Headlights crossed the front-room drapes as someone left or arrived.

Voices chimed in on "My Blue Heaven," died down during
"Moonlight in Vermont." Punchlines of jokes, shatter
of ice cubes from frozen slots, and someone

notorious for being madly in love with his wife
running across the room
to light her cigarette every time
she took one out of the pack.

The Fishing Trip

Speedometer rising on a flat straight stretch of Highway 16,
crowded-together lodgepole pines either side whiz by
the two-tone Olds 98, windy in back.
Dad adjusts the no-draft and Dogfish Woman
adjusts her crown of a shark's grin & fin, tarp
whumping the roof where lay the great blue tent
& hammers and pins to raise it, big top of summer
in whose gloom we blew up air mattresses,
dusty odour of rubber and sharp rings of the brass nipple
by the Kispiox where dogfish swam & prized sockeye
wriggled at the ends of poles and lines,
tourists filling ice chests with silver bodies of fish,
filleting them with sharp tools
at dusk, the frying pan, the sizzle above the blue flame
of the propane element. Fairy blue, uneven blue, hyacinth.

Anaïs Nin

Anaïs Nin's diaries much pondered, much
imitated — faux-exquisite phrasing
in lonely perplexed notebooks of Port Moody
trying to speak an intelligent womanhood —

My long cotton skirt, our
yellow canoe propped against the stucco

her Venetian masquerades &
libidinous houseboat on the Seine

her father in Brazilian tuxedos
mine singing "I Don't Want to Set the World on Fire"
in Ink Spots falsetto

her Henry Miller with manuscripts from Morocco

my *poète maudit* of the bookshelf,
snowplows outside his singularity,
his depressive realism. I could just see him
listening to *le jazz hot* as he clacked on a black Olivetti.

Robbie King
(1947–2003)

Robbie I remember you
coming over to the house for dinner
on West 6th near Balaclava,
one of those Mission-style bungalows
with the dark beams and built-ins
worth millions now, you'd have an ounce of coke
for my boyfriend Steve who took it
up one nostril then the other
morning, noon, and night from a tiny jade
jar on the dresser, there was no problem,
Steve was always kind and sweet and you
were polite & after awhile
throwing tremendous chords out the
upright as Steve counted
the measures & lifted his horn. Steve
careful on unaccustomed icy front steps
in ankle-length black leather coat and fedora,
ex-wife and daughter living on the North Shore,
red Alfa convertible parked on the street.
And you, Robbie, I'd hear your voice on the phone
and we'd laugh about something, but you were always
a bit distracted, a bit elsewhere, and I liked you
that way, stroking your mustache while I made steak
with Marchand de Vins Sauce from the Time-Life
French Provincial cookbook.

The Month of March

In the quiet hallway
outside my office door
reading a Gary Snyder poem
from a book I had in my briefcase
waiting for Security to let me back in
to my office for the car keys

while the dim afternoon wears on
in a palpable shedding of energy,
a droop of spirits, no sense
of anything new unlike Drake
(later to be Sir Francis)

in Snyder's poem coming across the
coast of California, light
brown and pine green, what is this, etc.,

up onto the beach, looking
around at the mountains &

a raincloud swiftly wedging into the valley
obscuring with chilly whiteness
the pines — winter's still with us

in that white hasty storm bending with old-fashioned
Siberian mind-power the grey metal of the parking lot
into cold hard cash.

The Consumptives at Tranquille Sanitorium, 1953

Gaunt hills
pine-dotted are the view
beyond the books propped
against the sun on the blanketed
laps of consumptives
taking the air.
Wild horses,
black cattle
cast shadows the
size of flies. Moving down
from winter shelter.

*

Bright blood startles white pans.
By green pastures,
the still waters, lambs of Jesus
rescued from tree limbs and
lightning. White beds,
white nurses, white
cream by the cupful.

*

Flies and hornets sidle against the screens
of verandas in the afternoon. Haze
and heat, doze and fever shudder. The book
falls to the lap. Across the lake, a horse
rubs against the soothing roughness
of a pine, releasing resin, retsina, plangent
wine of rembetika singers themselves
exiled and sometimes between acts
feverish on a shabby divan.

*

It's as quiet as the skin on a custard.
Gardeners clip and prune and feed.
Gladiolas' leek-like straight strong stalks
a reproach. The consumptives —
delicate, sensitive — victims of cities,
bad air, bad drains, bad
fiction, hard lives, a lack
of sunshine and morals.

*

Best they be housed far out of town
where their spit won't dry into dust
and then be blown into innocent
eyes and mouths when it gets hot out
& the wind leaps from side-streets.

*

Some of the nurses are not very happy.
Perhaps, not the cream of the crop? Forced
to these purposes: must have been forced —
or punished.
And disapproving of consumption,
though a charitable
intent to some degree could redeem
the situation. If a leper colony was
martyrdom, at least it was in Africa,
and had overtones.

*

In the heat of the afternoon, in the cold,
year after year the consumptives are wheeled out
to rest, to read on the veranda. And snooze
and doze. With double blankets and a hat
and red and seeping nose.

*

Early summer, fresh air flexing muscle.
Season of buttercups, green lawns,
tender vistas. A few cars coming in, going out.
On Sundays, children: some quiet, some exclaiming
as they gather for photos in the Sunken Garden.

*

A small crinkle-edge photo shows us
dressed up by a flowering shrub

— not recalling what I felt then, since my mother
being there had been gone and was still there &
gone.

*

Her dark hair grew longer. Her young life
grew older. I learned to read. I drew birds
in Art.

*

An array of consumptives, male and female,
young, old, natives from the Queen Charlottes
or up north, or dank Vancouver, or the War.
Nurses shook down thermometers, served
cupfuls of heavy cream and plenty of
eggs, eggs to the point of choking, also the cream.

*

Life was tranquil.
Effort discouraged. Patients gazed at the everlasting hills,
where cattle dispersed & returned.
Doctors, nurses, coroners, visitors
with lilac branches and gloves on, fear
of death palpable in the heat of the day,
the perfect climate: *better than Egypt* brayed
the local boosters.

*

Heat & radiation treatments shimmered
the lungs of the dying and the not-so-dead, a torrid dryness
camels could have plodded through,
saddles jingling with tambourines and laden with the rubies
of pomegranates, the oasis
where they kneel, where they are disburdened,
where they yawn and show their shocking teeth.

Oyama Pink Shale

A pinkish glow
beyond the curve of the highway, beyond

dark weird knobs of tilted earth and veils of yellowy grass
companion'd by vast turquoise of lake —

and in gravel pits and mounds in the garden centres
crushed pieces of peach-pink shale like tablets of blush
in brass-hinged compacts

for borders and backdrops, to set off
the complexions of tall, creamy yuccas

guarding the front yard of Pluto's gloom
far below from whence a slight knocking

sound can be heard, as of someone wanting out.

The Mummy Suite

1.

The sheet-clad customer stares into the mirror
unaware of himself, tufts of cut-off
grey-brown hair littering his shoulders. The barber
moves around like a dance partner,
elbow nudging the razor cord away then crouching
to tidy behind his ears, arms sheeted like the stiffness of mummies
staggering down the street while citizens scatter
and the horns of their cars get stuck
— cars by now on top of one another on the sunny
ordinary day mummies decide to remind the citizens of their
oldtime curses from the tombs of yesteryear at the matinee —
Tony's getting old, the shop frayed & frazzled, his wife dead —
everything's worse, the mummies drive by in Ford 350 pickups
    trailing
invisible bandages & wearing large gold bracelets.

2.

Mercury dashes, Venus trots around the sun,
a girl in a yellow dress. Earth saunters,
Neptune appears stationary. The human orrery performs
the clock of the solar system upon the grass of the commons.
Magnetisms and attractions keep them circling
one another as brittle & old-fashioned
as when people were repressed. Pluto is
way over in the parking lot. Across
the highway, like a stone spit from a tire,
the spacecraft Voyager. Voyager
sits in the void slowly and rapidly
somersaulting towards its destination.
Old sputniks whiz by with their mummified pilots
like the celestial barques of Ra. Mars
stomps around red-faced,
Uranus squires his pretty moon.

3.

Once they got there, they enjoyed
the natural hot springs that
leaked sulphur into the air, but healing sulphur.
Rheumatoids, the thyroid-deficient, the easily
startled found the waters soothing. Hades chuckled
beneath their aching feet, sent up bubbles and
shots of steam. They kept an eye
out for bears and hippie mommies
dreadlocked and braless still nursing aged
articulate toddlers. They felt old.

Brightness fell upon the cedar boughs
the hippies stroked themselves with when they
rose streaming from the steam, and brightness fell
upon the bronze fur of grizzly bears
hoping someone would drop their egg sandwich.

The World

The world was bisected by a river
the dog would swim as a god moves
between realms: the floor, the air, the tanbark, the ceiling
of the big top. The hero poses in white tights
on a small diving board up high, gauging
the space: oh, if only God were an angel!

The band starts up a bravura refrain.
A tall clown speeds in a midget car to a gas pump.
A huge foot emerges, the clown unfolds, the gas
a spigot the clown presses his big white hand over
to no avail. The wrong lever is pressed, someone is shot
skyward, geysers erupt, a clerk is clobbered.

Several cops dash in from the wings, sirens sound,
king-size welts emerge from
foreheads. Up above in the spotlit gloom of
the big top, trim and fit in a '50s way, he touches
briefly his heart and leaves the ladder for the air.

The Big Top

With both a foot and a hand
on the bar I reach out over the abyss to Burt Lancaster
who will meet me in the middle, grasping my hand
with his whole hand and wrist reinforced by a wide cuff
he pulled on thoughtfully in his dressing room prior
to the show.
And I let go. Trust is the real plot
of ground hence the gap between man and God
on the ceiling, the colour of the sky not even changing,
blue as ever, clouds, but too high for birds, while Burt
slips into his slippers and rubs his palms with gripping powder.

The Nets of Being

> *Awake, my sleeping ones, I cry out to you,*
> *disentangle the nets of being!*
>
> Charles Olson, "As the Dead Prey Upon Us"

> *The net can be very dangerous.*
>
> Tito Gaona, aerialist, Ringling Brothers Circus

An array of hairnets — the hairnets of Jove's wife
& those who work in the kitchens of Jove

placing feet on filament horizontals
climbing *each step of the ladders*

into the firmament
along the length of a sunset's greenish horizon

in the space of the big top
one makes the catch, another, the throw

the grip, brother to brother, was phenomenal,
for the triple mid-air somersault

he climbed the twenty-one Lucite rungs
of the slender rope ladder with an aerialist's

sideways climb, each slippered foot placed
around a siderope onto a rung

his brother already waiting
hanging upside down

the feat applauded by janitors and clowns
the afternoon of rehearsal, each knot

of the net below its own particular fire
welding the wounds of separation
as smudges of the dead return grabbing

the instants which were not lived

#'s of sunrises, #'s of people and
personality types going to work in the kitchens

and sweatshops of cosmos stitching
fast the seams of flailing garments

flung down toward the next
step in the track of making,
each dangling thread

particular as the leavings of a beard in the sink,
pennants of DNA in the slight moons of clipped nails

stray strands tucked into the shower caps of the kids
making computers and cell phones
in moon suits, the moon's white bone

catches the reflection of tossed pebbles,
the corner of a floating net, a knot
untying, a stray strand escaping,

hyacinth sunrise of fire opal a far-off vent
of breath & peace carved out from

*the mammothness of the comings & goings
of the ladders of life*

*

one had her hair plaited
to the harness she hung from

to avoid the burn of the nets
below *which could really hurt*

she juggled flaming torches
she did multiple rapid body spins

one day her hair unknotted
and she fell to the tanbark, having said
no net I am fastened by my hair
to the air

and broke her neck but lived

*the nets which entangle us are flames
spread out across each plane of being*

*

back in some *histoire d'amour*
a pair of laddered stockings is laid aside

a world is coloured
by jars of licorice, banded pigeons, soft-hued parasols,

firefly sparks and embroidery hoops make up a day
stitched to sadness by a stray song

winter furs so cold the various pellicules stand out
like the faint beard of a Viking woman

#'s of iron filings hopelessly in love
with a toy magnet, a tilted globe spinning to indicate

the magnificent travel plans of railway plutocrats
puffed up in furs and feathers

alighting in foreign lands to fezzes and muezzins
camels kneeling and rising laden with women

insomniacs, black circles under their eyes,
dead souls, some record playing on the victrola,

silhouettes, flakes of poppy, tassles
softly sweeping away a dream

*

black hair, blind dark, tantalizing tangle
of flecks and #'s of luminous horizons

take your pick: the pebble, the funnel, the nest,
the vitreous floater beneath frosted blue eye shadow

the small black hole or the oval sky-blue vent
the stitched, the laced, the #'s of gems, the debris

of ourselves, flakes and lashes, rashes
caught in the trammels, *the multiple nets.*

*

Slender beings laced into sparking spangles ascend, descend

one the flier, one the catcher, one
spins by the hair juggling several flaming torches

another below, lancing a blister with a heated hatpin,
the unguent warm spread of its water across

the palm of a hand that had gripped the bar
in the spotlit dark of the big top

as angels and demons and men
go up and down

2 horses run around with one rider straddling both
2 clowns drive a tiny car at top speed honking

what wind clears the sodden weight of goods & equipments
let none of the threads be left upon the earth

let there be only paradise

*

going to get our stitches out following grids
of streets and traffic, appointments, #'s of duties

we examine the new scar's border of threads
& unravel filaments of time, #'s of memories

bunched up in nerve fibres clinging together
like the rubber tires which in Olson's dream

looked as though they only needed air,
the rear tires *masses of rubber & thread*

clear dawning breaks through the deep bruise of night
a remnant of mesh floats away on the breeze

*

bone-coloured cloud, sparks from the campfire,
beach pebbles laid out as discrete thoughts

as sun goes down and stars come up
a dark train speeds along black tracks

the black tracks are left hot
the opal moon rises

a mesh of static spread out,
Andromeda ticking and whooshing

like the bloodstream, inconstant,
melodic, secret —

antennae tweaked to cosmos
where the threads of life are snipped

and left in tiny piles as below the chair of the barber
the brunette leavings of the customer now paying

lie, and the customer among #'s of customers
returns to work, dons a hairnet,

shoves down into the deep fryer the mesh pan
cold bone-white shards criss-cross

arrayed like martyrs in vegetable surrender
to *the nets we are entangled in*

*

sparks of stars in space debris
subducted bonfires of the actual

the nets which entangle us are flames
Olson writes, having looked up the Five Hindrances

under "Buddhism" in the *Encyclopedia Britannica*,
writing *to alleviate the dream*

writing to alleviate poetry, the mother, the beam
of the projector in the darkened living room

the spotlight that finds the catcher hanging upside down
not by his knees from the catchbar

but with the ropes that support the bar wrapped
tightly around his legs, *o souls, in life and in death*

catcher and flyer grip each other's wrists
and hold on tight

and that's when the janitors and clowns
came racing out shouting and clapping

the night in Tucson Miguel Vasquez
turned over four times in mid-air

into the hands of his brother Juan
at just that moment before I really start to fall

he said, *I float there for a second
and my brother caught me at just that moment*

*

threaded filaments through
the eye of cosmic sewing

stitching the wounds of separation
knitting a nexus of filaments, nests, nets

a knot loosened, an end dangling
pulled through history

a woman sewing a button on a cuff
breaks the thread with her teeth

young girls stitch furiously in factories
in textile dust 24/7 opalescent fabrics

mauve, orange, azure blue
sunrise a memory, #'s of black patterns

strewn like the petals of a starburst
and you wonder, do they think

the fabrics are beautiful, do they crave them
as what slides through their authentic hands

is a mauveness matching the circles under their eyes
or an azure blue the colour of eternal rest.

Lines

Those were lines I thought worthy
of her *intelletto*: a word Michelangelo used,
or was used about him. And it's not just
intellect.

Now I realize how hard it is to change
the habits of a lifetime. Like not
saying anything makes of my mouth
a line. I should just relax.

This fall I won't bother buying new boots.
And in my classes screw it I'll simply intuit
what needs doing next.

I'll take a pass on today's trip to the river.
Won't be dipped, nor help dip
anyone else in it, though we all
could use salvation

& I can still remember the busy angel
in my dream, the knife-sharp pleats
of her white linen dress, blazing white,
chic, and her narrow foreign face: she handed me
something and took off in a hurry.

Rosary beads, handed to me by an angel!
It was definitely the sort of dream you remember
or write down in a leather journal.

I liked that she was a busy woman,
had no time for wisdoms and hugs. Just the beads,
the hurry, and the sharp folds.

Queen of the North

U-Hauls, Safeway semis, all-purpose delivery trucks
lashed by ropes
to hooks in the wall of the hull below —

Cars crammed in down there together all
facing the same direction
like soldiers quietly inside the Trojan Horse

for passage across Hecate Strait one hundred
miles over shallow nasty seas to Haida Gwaii

seven hours, what is an hour to a gull or
a killer whale but to us there were seven
as horizons fell and rose

& passengers dozed in dimmed corridors.

The boat felt old, in the hands of lunatics or ghost
mariners from an unknown narrative. I figured it would be
    a wonder
if we ever returned from this Return Trip

before she'd veer toward
an isle called Gil that would breach
the very hull where our autos lay bewitched
between her bones that tilt and settle deeper still.

The Middle of August

Longer shadows across the road, tree boughs
huff in breezes, Oyama pink shale pale
and perverse.

The last of the hummingbirds air-raids
a syrupy red feeder now busy with a row of ants.

The news issues from the radio & an
element's on medium-high

for one of my burned and briny dinners. According
to the pundits of cosmos the Perseid Showers

are announcing a major event in Ursa Minor
and I'm holding pieces of a minor animal in tongs —

its sides and middle, its wings and thighs, once
so cute and peeping in the incubator
at Buckerfield's in the spring.

February

Moods and woes, clank and drag,
    snow shovels, tire tracks at busy angles
        where someone was towed from the ditch.

Sudden snow storm, dry and distracted.
    rounded V of deer hooves from dawn foragings,
        trot of coyote tracks lines of hunger in the deeper snow.

Figures waver in the fog ahead.
    A way-too-big house being built sits alone.

Airplanes strain toward Cancun

but I like it here where dirty cars idle at traffic lights
    & pallid Valentine's shoppers tiptoe over beige slush

to purchase in the Humour section
    chastening truths re. the body's dismay.

Life Studies

Light is prefigured by singing
    the morning's delightful raiment and complexity —
        leaf, wind, scent

the breeze a plank for a blackbird
    in the wetlands
        I have no line

behind an effigy of "self"
    oh doctor of philosophy
        prescribing all kinds of nutty stuff makes us no less

mentally ill
    going up and down the streets with an air
        of destination, faking it

    nowhere to go
        nowhere to be

but pass the day naked
    and hidden
        all eyes and crabwise movement.

The Torturer's Horse

For once I'm not so ordinary as to
stop the dog barking at the neighbour's
three-year old. He sings
on his tricycle, back and forth
across the deck, a private song.
The late-summer sun glares *as it must*
over the now-silent child, pedalling away.
The lake is mint-blue and gallant with craft
despite the calm day, horse latitudes
of stillness, the many flight paths
overhead. No doubt envy is part
of the story too, along with the crying geese,
the horse's behind, the family dynamics.

No one looks up at airplanes anymore
unless they fly too low over the pitch 'n putt,
the outdoor market with its carrots
and birdhouses. And how the abacus
of suffering takes its place alongside
the other types of calculation, the palm readers,
the circus riders three abreast on their steeds
in the picture book the child takes to his nap.

A Lovely Day

Plump white clouds, a nice breeze. Not a scorcher, not one you'd
mind in any way. I found a near-new softball at the park
this morning behind the dugout & holding its white weight
in my palm remembered
days on the diamond with the Cosmic League

& summer nights at Riverview Park
when Dad pitched for the Royalite team
& my happiness when he struck out player
after player as the light in the hills began to
remove itself from the scoreboard and the skirts of
the weeping willows
blew about in the night breeze.

White Hillside

Long light falls across long grasses —
tresses of marmots combed out
like a hold-up artist's wildeyed wig.

In "Hlagwajiina and His Family" Ghandl says
from their burrows the marmots could see shadows
of hands. Deadfalls bore the details of their housepoles.

Hills are happy drawings: mounds dotted with trees,
or not, naked mounds. Some knobby,
carbuncular, bent sideways like pound cake batter
frozen in mid-whip from when the earth tipped
& twirled & gravity liquefied beneath the winds
let loose. Within human memory, the ur-trauma.

Some say, 800 mph winds.

Rintrah roars and shakes his fires in the burden'd air.

Best not suspend anyone's head, the story goes,
for a being from the sea could just flip
the town over. Failing that, strike it
with a red stick. The town shuddered & shook.

Designs on the deadfalls were to call the marmots,
but when one marmot went out for a look — as you do
when it comes to design —
he was caught by hunters. The rest of the marmots
watched from inside the corridors of their burrow
among nettle roots, being missing people
who wear copper necklaces.

Death in the Moonlight, a Sinking Canoe

light overtook him
and folded up time

It began to take on water.
    More water. Now
        Sinking, far, far from shore.

Smoke-green alpine lake
    An icy lead-coloured sheen in the night.

On the railway side a high black bank.
    Opposite: coves, curves, twinkling lights.
        Who wouldn't try to swim there instead?

Even though it was the longer way.

From Toledo

Spring: that far-off moment!

For now, a light rain pesters
a sepia scene. I run upstairs
from unrolling a mauve shag rug
to find at the door a young woman
delivering flowers — an autumnal
arrangement, dark reds,
deep yellows. Her
white happy van drives off. I brush
mauve fluff from my hands and
slip *The Song of the Sibyl* into the player.
Its plangent notes occupy
the cavernous cathedral.

The Sybil: a boy wearing a wig,
a tunic, & *a hairy tail which gives him
the appearance of a mermaid.*
The Procession of Prophets
laments the Day of Judgement,
the splitting & rending of the world,
a piece of old blue and white cloth in the righteous
hands of Wrath. Puffs of dust
rise from the rip lines.

*

From Toledo, the Spanish town
in whose cathedral the Sybil sang
I have a pair of brass scissors inlaid
with a scrolling pattern. The cathedral
one of many we visited that year, that
decade — the decade of the pewter goblet
received for years of service, now stored
in its lizardy protective case.

The Sybil's song takes me to poetry,
that coughing sister, the one in bed
using up her sick days. A soft old cloth
folded and warmed in the oven

is pressed like a benediction
to her Vicks-slick chest.

*

Years of service at the blackboard
diagramming this or that situation
with spirals and connotations. Are all interpretations
a matter of possibilities endlessly recycled
within the one Possibility: our human life on the earth.
As some might say, within Creation.

Imperial trumpets announce their own representations
of pagan intrusion, pagan self-esteem. Uh-oh,
here we go.

*

When it comes to the Sybil, we cannot be too
walking-on-eggshells. A boy in sleeves and gloves.

She/he emerges, sings, leaves
the scene or is absorbed in many cowed
and repentant voices.

Her/his mantilla, cloak, jewels,
gown, the cloth at the waist are
a folded dimension aslant her sightlines.

*

Amens signal her departure & the arrival
of the next prophet. The congregation
has been waiting a long time for the newer music,
the variations, the brow-furrowing
interpretations, the standing up, the tired choir,
the always-already moment, its lauded shine.

The Shepherdess
A painting in oils, 1899

Preceding her, a dozen or so greyish sheep.
Clayey puddles gleam in ruts, scrub bush
vague on the horizon. Dark red, dark blue
her vestments: a holy thing, the hour.
The activity. Even the farthest-to-the-left
sheep holds dear to the flock.

Her switch is benign, nearly forgotten.
They are being led out to pasture.
Why would anyone just take off, or be bad?

The sky is a large creamy portion, nor star nor planet
visible. Dew-soaked chilly grass. As yet,
immanence reigns. It moves softly forward,
it speaks in bleats. The shepherdess is silent, accustomed.

Every morning he turns away from the view
and toward his easel. A few years later
someone will mention he married
a woman he met on the train at the moment
it crossed the River Wye.

But now it is only the River When that he thinks about.
And the old pale colours of the land.

Notes and Acknowledgements

The epigraph is from Etel Adnan's *The Indian Never Had a Horse* (Sausalito, CA: Post-Apollo Press, 1985).

Versions of the following poems have been published elsewhere, and with thanks to their editors: "The Consumptives at Tranquille Sanitorium, 1953" was published by *The Capilano Review*; "From Toledo" was published as a chapbook by Barry McKinnon's Gorse Press; "Ripple Rock" and "Queen of the North" were published in *Okanagan Arts* magazine. "The Nets of Being" was written as captions for a series of paintings called "Targeting Light Sources" by Marion Llewellyn. A chapbook presenting the poem along with reproductions of some of the paintings was designed by Marion Llewellyn and published by Dream Dead Press. The poem was also published by *Event* magazine.

I borrowed and adapted some of the images in the poem "White Hillside" from Ghandl's *Nine Visits to the Myth World*, translated by Robert Bringhurst. The reference to the cremation of the pets in "Graphite" I gratefully owe to Gillian Wigmore. In "Bracelet," the carver whose signature is "XX" is Victor Adams. John Culhane's *The American Circus* provided information about the Ringling Bros.' productions.

"Robbie King" is about Robbie's friendship with Steve Douglas, who lived in Vancouver in the 1970s. Robbie played the Hammond B3 organ in dozens of Vancouver venues to wild acclaim, and for many years would grace a set now and then at the Yale Hotel. He passed away in 2003. Steve Douglas, saxophonist and flautist, passed away in Los Angeles in 1993 while warming up for a recording session with Ry Cooder. In 2003 Steve Douglas was inducted into the Rock and Roll Hall of Fame.

"Death in the Moonlight, a Sinking Canoe" is for my beloved nephew Tyler Thesen, who drowned in Alta Lake in Whistler, B.C., in 2003.

Thank you to the Faculty of Creative and Critical Studies at UBC Okanagan who awarded me Faculty Support funds for Leighton Studio residencies at the Banff Centre; to Patricia Young, Jenny Penberthy, and Diana Hartog for their generous advice on the manuscript; to Nancy Holmes, Heidi Garnett, and Lindsay Diehl for their company and conversation; and to my husband Paul Mier for his enduring and endearing encouragement. And especially, thank you to Ken Babstock for the kindness, wit, and poetic intelligence he brought to the editing process.

This book is dedicated to Robin Blaser (1925–2009), longtime friend and "companion of the way."

> *each of us a warm fragment*
> *broken off from the greater*
> *ornament of the unseen*
> *then rejoined as dust*
> *to all this is.*
> — Jimmy Santiago Baca

AUTHOR PHOTOGRAPH: BUD MORTENSON

About the Author

SHARON THESEN's books of poems include *Aurora, News & Smoke* (selected poems), *A Pair of Scissors*, and *The Good Bacteria*. She grew up in small towns across western Canada and lived in Vancouver for many years, where she taught at Capilano College and was an editor of *The Capilano Review*. She now lives near Kelowna, B.C., and teaches in the Department of Creative Studies at UBC's Okanagan campus.